KITCHEN HACKS

The Ultimate Collection Of Secrets, Tips and Tricks

Katie Mankoff & Adam Mankoff

Copyright

Disclaimer

The information contained in this work is for general information purposes only. The information is provided by ILKEM LLC and while ILKEM LLC endeavors to keep the information accurate and correct, ILKEM LLC makes no representations or warranties of any kind, express or implied, about the completeness, accuracy, reliability, suitability or availability with respect to the work or the information, products, services, or related graphics contained in the work for any purpose. Any reliance you place on such information is therefore strictly at your own risk.

In no event will ILKEM LLC, the authors, or publisher be liable for any loss or damage including without limitation, indirect or consequential loss or damage, or any loss or damage whatsoever arising from loss of data or profits arising out of, or in connection with, the use of this work. The authors, publisher, and ILKEM LLC specifically claim no responsibility for any liability, loss, or risk, personal or otherwise, which is incurred as a consequence, directly or indirectly, of the use and application of any of the contents of this book.

Dedication: This book is dedicated with love to the greatest family in the world: Curt, Linda, JJ, Patti, Melissa, Tania, John, Jen, Jack and Big.

Intro

Meet your new best friend in the kitchen, **Kitchen Hacks.** You won't ever cook without it by your side! To maximize learning, approach these ideas with the eagerness of a newbie and the willingness to try new things. Instantly improve your skills in the kitchen, regardless of your experience, and prepare to better yourself with an open mind. Now let's have fun, make great food, and get started!

Table Of Contents

Appetizers

1. **How Much To Make:** Throwing a dinner party with refreshments before the meal? The rule of 4 to 6 hors d'oeuvres per person should work. If it's cocktails only, plan for 8 to 10 hors d'oeuvres per person.

2. **No-Cook Success:** Don't have time to cook? Set out cheeses, simple spreads and bread, crackers, and cut veggies. Get creative with presentation, such as serving spinach dip in a bread bowl.

3. **Colors Of The Rainbow:** When making a veggie tray, think color. A mixture of red, yellow, and green is much more fun than veggies all the same color.

4. **No-Wash Bowls:** To serve dips, hollow out bell peppers or use bread bowls. When finished, no need to wash. Simply eat or throw away!

5. **Free Your Fridge:** Planning to have a party with appetizers? Clean out the fridge the day before to ensure you have adequate storage space. Use an ice chest for additional space if needed.

6. **Variety Is Best:** When hosting a party with appetizers as the main food, be sure to provide a variety. Keep in mind guests who may need low-calorie, kosher, diabetic, gluten-free, or vegetarian options.

7. **Helpful Warnings:** If you are serving appetizers with common allergens such as peanuts and shellfish, be sure to warn your guests. Cute tags can be added to the serving trays that say "Made with Peanuts," etc.

8. **Stereotypes And Such:** When preparing your appetizers, consider your guest list. Younger guests will likely eat more, and older guests will usually limit themselves to just a few. Active party games may create a need for more hearty food choices.

9. **Small Servings**: Appetizers are meant to be small and eaten on the move. If utensils are required, it's not an appetizer.
10. **Cold, Warm, And Hot**: Running out of food is a party-killer. Make sure there is always food available by having a cold appetizer, a room-temperature appetizer, and a hot one.
11. **Money Misers**: Appetizers are great money-saving foods for parties. You only need small amounts of ingredients for each serving. You can get almost 30 small pieces of toast from one baguette! Spend less on the main course by filling your guests up with appetizers.
12. **Lost Beverages**: Typically drinks accompany appetizers. To help guests keep from misplacing their beverages, give them wine charms or personalized beverage holders as a nice touch. There are some great ideas on Pinterest.
13. **Chill The Wine**: Like your wine chilled? Freeze grapes and use them to keep wine chilled in your glass without adding water, which tends to dilute the taste.
14. **Dried Up**: Making dried tomatoes for your appetizer is not hard, but does take time. Cut lengthwise and place on an oiled or parchment-lined baking sheet in an oven preheated to 190 degrees F. Allow about 10 hours for drying. Let cool and then sprinkle with sea salt and/or olive oil and store in a glass jar in the fridge.
15. **Tea Sandwiches**: Have fun by coloring cream cheese in pretty pastel colors for tea sandwiches. Use just a few drops of food coloring and blend. Add some sugar and vanilla for a little sweetness.

Baking

1. **Towel It**: Grease baking pans using a paper towel. Rub a little bit of shortening or butter along all areas of the pan (if the recipe calls for a greased pan).
2. **Baking Utensils**: Make sure you have both liquid and dry measuring spoons and cups, and the specified pan sizes. Recipes require a standard dry-measuring cup for dry ingredients, which include flours, cocoa powder, granulated (brown and regular) sugar, cornmeal, and powdered sugars.
3. **Tricks Of The Shell**: Fingers aren't good for retrieving eggshells. When eggshell pieces fall in the batter or mixture, use the empty half-shell to scoop them out.
4. **Rack Rules**: Wondering which oven rack to use? The middle rack is the best choice for baking unless otherwise specified.
5. **Pie Preparation**: If baking more than one pie, lower your oven temperature. If the 2 pies are different, use the lowest oven temperature of the two recipes. Bake on separate baking sheets.
6. **Don't Go Changing**: When baking, don't change the recipe. Cooking can be modified, but baking is an exact science.
7. **Only the Best:** You get out what you put in. Use the freshest dairy, fruits, and spices to give the best baking results.
8. **Beating Basics:** Don't over-beat or under-beat your cake batter or you risk changing the cake's texture or volume. One minute of mixer beating time is the same as 150 strokes by hand.
9. **Best Eggs**: Unless a baking recipe calls for a specific size of egg, choose medium to large. Large eggs can cause cakes to fall while cooling.
10. **Shine On:** Shiny aluminum pans reflect heat away. When baking cakes this will result in a soft, golden crust.

11. **Chocolaty Dust**: When a recipe calls for dusting the tins with flour, try something tastier instead - use a little of the dry cake mix or sifted cocoa powder.
12. **Cracking Up**: Does your cake crack when baking? This means your oven is too hot or the rack is placed too high in the oven.
13. **Baking Powder Basics**: Did you know baking powder loses its strength? Test yours - pour hot water into a small bowl and add 1 teaspoon of your baking powder. It should fizz like crazy. If it doesn't, it needs to be replaced.
14. **Butter Means Butter**: Butter, margarine, and shortening are often not interchangeable in recipes. The fats are different and may change the result of the recipe.
15. **Extract Or Flavoring**: What's the difference? Extracts are required to contain the natural flavor. Flavorings and imitations may be made artificially.
16. **Cold Concoctions**: When using extracts for cooking, add them when your mixture is cold. If added when the mixture is hot, some flavor may be lost due to evaporation.
17. **Pack It In**: Brown sugar should be measured by packing it in a dry-cup measure, whether specified or not. With brown sugar, packing is always assumed.
18. **Trade-Off Cakes**: Missing the right size cake pan? Two 8-inch square baking pans will work instead of a 13 x 9-inch baking pan.
19. **No Peeking**: Don't open the oven door while your desserts are baking. Each peek lets out 20% or more of the heat.
20. **Repurposed Tools**: A chopstick or broken kitchen tool handle can be stored in the flour container as a measuring cup level. This prevents dirtying another utensil each time.
21. **Cool Off**: Run out of cooling rack space for pies? Use an upside-down muffin pan as an extra cooling rack. The middle space between molds allows free airflow.

22. **Parchment Pointer**: When rolling piecrust, place dough between 2 sheets of parchment or waxed paper. This avoids the flour mess and makes for a more tender crust.

23. **True Trifecta**: Chocolate, vanilla, and salt are made for each other. Use vanilla to give chocolate a smooth taste, and salt to enhance the chocolate taste and balance the natural sweetness.

24. **Muffin Mastery**: If you want your muffins to slide from the pan without sticking, place the hot pan on a wet towel first. They should slide right out.

25. **Take The Cake**: For parties, don't pre-slice your cake more than 20 minutes ahead or the cake will dry out.

26. **Embrace The Brown**: When bananas turn brown, don't toss them out. Peel and freeze them to use in banana bread later.

27. **Bounty Of Berries**: Buy berries in season at a cheaper price. Freeze them on a cookie sheet and then place in zippered freezer bags. You'll have perfectly frozen individual berries rather than a mushy mess.

28. **Soaking For Success**: If raisins are called for in a recipe, try plumping them first. Measure the amount of raisins required by the recipe, cover with very hot water (not boiling) and allow them to soak and plump for 2 to 5 minutes.

29. **Rockin' Raisins**: Try soaking raisins in cola instead of water. Cola plumps them up and adds a delicious spiciness.

30. **Raisin Ratio**: Raisins often sink to the bottom of the cake batter. When adding raisins to batter, stir only 1/4 of the recipe amount into the batter. Pour the batter into your pan and top it with the reserved raisins.

31. **Floating Fruit**: When making blueberry muffins, toss fresh blueberries with a tablespoon of flour to keep them from sinking to the bottom. The flour helps them stick to the batter.

Beans

16. **Soak It**: Most beans must be soaked before cooking. Generally they should soak a minimum of four hours to ensure a shorter cooking time and prevent a loss of nutrients.
17. **Skip The Soak**: Some beans are ready to cook and don't require soaking. If you want to cook right away, choose lentils or split peas.
18. **Save The Salt**: When cooking a pot of beans, wait until they are fully cooked before salting them. Salting early in the cooking process can harden the beans.
19. **Thin Beans**: If your pot of beans is too watery and thin, remove 1/2 cup of beans, mash them in a small bowl, pour them back into the pot, and stir to thicken.
20. **Toss The Water**: Throw out the water used to soak your beans and then use fresh water to cook them. This will reduce the risk of intestinal gas.

Breads

1. **Crisp Or Soft Crust**: For bread, using water in the recipe makes a crispier crust. If you prefer a softer crust, use milk instead.

2. **Beating The Brown**: If your bread is browning too much in your oven, remove it and make a tent over the loaf with aluminum foil to shield it from direct heat. Return to the oven to finish baking.

3. **Healthy Eggs**: Want bread that's lower in cholesterol and fat? To reduce these unhealthy ingredients, substitute 2 egg whites for a whole egg.

4. **Flour Fouls**: Self-rising and all-purpose flours are not equal. Self-rising flour includes salt and baking powder. To make your own, add 1 cup all-purpose flour to 1-1/2 teaspoons baking powder and 1/2 teaspoon salt.

5. **Youthful Yeast**: When buying, check the expiration date and always select the freshest available. Yeast loses its strength over time, resulting in delayed rising times.

6. **Foamy Proof**: If you have active dry yeast, "proof" it to tell if it's active. To do this, take 1/4 cup warm water, add 2-1/4 teaspoons yeast and 1 teaspoon sugar, then allow the mixture to sit for 5-10 minutes. If it foams, it's good; if not, throw it away.

7. **Bread Holes**: Does your bread have unwanted holes in it? This is a result of the air not being pressed out before forming the loaf or from allowing the dough to rise too long.

8. **Doughy Bottom**: Don't leave bread in pans to cool. Always remove from pans and place on cooling racks after baking so air can circulate and prevent sogginess.

9. **Slow The Slice**: Don't cut freshly baked bread too soon. Doing so may negatively alter the texture. Cool it for at least 2 hours before slicing if in a rush, but resting it overnight is recommended.

10. **Freezer Over Fridge**: Keeping your bread in the refrigerator will make it hard. It will stay fresh up to 3 months if kept in the freezer and then thaw to a softer texture.
11. **Tasty Toppings**: Before baking bread, add some tasty toppings. Brush dough with oil or water and then sprinkle on sunflower seeds or other grains for texture and taste.
12. **Similar But Not Equal**: If you're using a bread maker, do not use recipes intended for the oven, and vice versa.
13. **Experiment With Flavor**: Try tossing some flavorful additions in your dough. Foods like olives, bacon bits, and cheese all bake nicely in a loaf of bread. Avoid additions that contain a lot of water.
14. **Keep It Fresh**: When possible, use freshly ground wheat. This makes for softer bread that is more nutritious.
15. **Salt And Yeast**: When combining ingredients, don't combine salt and yeast alone ahead of time. They don't play nicely together unless they have flour to help.
16. **Just Right**: When developing your yeast, use hot water. If you can hold your finger in it comfortably, it's not too hot.
17. **Keep It Kosher**: If you use kosher salt in your bread recipe, you need to adjust the quantity. Use about 1/2 teaspoon less than most recipes call for, unless kosher salt is specified.

Breakfast

1. **Fabulous French Toast**: French toast is all about the bread. Experiment with breads other than white, such as Texas toast, whole grain, and oat-nut varieties.

2. **Mixture Medleys**: When mixing the egg and milk mixture for French toast, add in a little sugar and vanilla for some extra sweetness. Cinnamon is a good addition too.

3. **Stale Suggestion**: Fresh white bread can fall apart easily with heavy French toast coating. Try using the more stale pieces of bread that will withstand the extra weight and moisture.

4. **Perfect-Size Pancakes**: Re-purpose an empty ketchup bottle by using it for pouring pancake batter. The squirt nozzle allows you to dispense just the right amount of batter into the pan with no drips.

5. **Baked Bacon**: Cook bacon on a pan in a 400 degree F oven for 10 minutes to get it evenly done. There will also be less to clean after.

6. **Flat Bacon**: To lessen curling bacon, dip it in cold water before cooking.

Butter

1. **Soften Butter Fast**: If your recipe calls for softened butter, use a cheese grater to shred cold butter into pieces that will soften quickly.
2. **Spread It On**: If you need softened butter to spread on bread quickly, place a warmed bowl or pan over the butter dish. The butter will be soft in no time.
3. **Friendly Fat**: If a recipe calls for butter or margarine, do not use low-fat versions. They won't work as well as the real thing.

Candy

1. **Weather Warning**: Before making candy, check the weather forecast. Sunny and dry days are great for candy making, but rain and high humidity can cause setting problems.
2. **Thermometer Tactics**: For candy making, get a good candy thermometer. You can make candy without one, but it's harder for beginners in particular. One with a metal clamp that clips on the pan is helpful.
3. **Test Time**: Always test that your thermometer is accurate. Place in a boiling pan of water to check the temperature. It should be 212 degrees F. Adjust cooking as necessary.
4. **Measure Before Mixing**: Measure out all candy making ingredients beforehand. Getting the temperature to 220 degrees F takes a while, but you want to have everything ready when it hits that point.
5. **Flat-Bottom Pans**: When melting sugars, use a heavy-duty saucepan with a flat bottom. This will help prevent scorching.
6. **Low And Slow**: Dissolve your sugar into the liquid ingredients over low heat, and then slowly bring to a boil. Once dissolved, don't stir the sugar mixture unless indicated by the recipe.
7. **Dry It Out**: You don't want moisture in your sugar. One good way to absorb any extra moisture in your sugar container is to dry it for a few hours in a container with a desiccant packet.
8. **Sugar Burns**: The temperature of sticky, boiled sugar can exceed 320 degrees F. The human body temperature is about 98.6 degrees F. Ouch!
9. **Attention Please:** Candy making deserves your undivided attention. For safety reasons, ban the kids and pets from the room to avoid distractions.
10. **Protect The Fingers**: Always use a wooden spoon greased with oil to stir the melting sugar mixture. The oil helps

prevent sticking. A metal handle gets too hot and can burn your hands.

11. **Steam Burns Too**: When sugar syrups bubble up, they make a lot of very hot steam. Adding creams and other ingredients makes it worse. Wear oven mitts that cover hands and forearms, and hold the pan far from your face when pouring.

12. **Super Sugar**: When making candy, always use a fresh, unopened package of sugar to ensure purity.

13. **Save The Salt**: When making candy, use unsalted butter unless the recipe says otherwise. Unsalted butter is fresher than salted butter and gives better results.

14. **Scorching Is A Sign**: If you cannot stir your sugar mixture before it scorches on the bottom, your burner is turned too high. There's no great fix for this, so toss it out and start fresh at a lower temperature.

15. **Size Matters**: Use the specific size pan called for in the recipe. Using a different size can alter the cooking time and impact the results.

16. **Double Is Trouble**: Unless you are a candy making pro, don't try to double a recipe to save time. Making separate batches will ensure the ingredients are correct for the designated cooking time.

17. **Mixing It Up**: When you need to melt chocolate with water or other liquid, combine them at the start of the melting process. This will keep the chocolate from turning gritty.

18. **Oven-Melted Chocolate**: Put minced chocolate in a metal bowl then place it in the oven. The temperature should be set to 110 degrees or at the lowest temperature setting (with the door slightly open). The chocolate will melt in about 60 minutes.

19. **Take A Dip**: Make a dipping chocolate coating for candies and other treats by adding 1 tablespoon vegetable oil to 6 - 8 ounces of solid chocolate and melting them together.

20. **Super Storage**: All kinds of chocolate need proper storage to avoid absorbing other odors. Wrap it tightly and store at around 65 - 68 degrees F and about 50% humidity to keep it good for almost six months. Dark chocolate can last longer.
21. **No Scraping**: It's tempting to scrape every fudgy bit from the sides of your saucepan or bowl, but don't. It will make the fudge too gritty.
22. **Beat The Blooms:** Chocolate can "bloom" when stored at temperatures warmer than 75 degrees F. A white cocoa butter film may develop on the surface. It doesn't look great, but it's safe to eat.
23. **Fine Like Wine**: Dark chocolate is an amazing confection. It contains healthy antioxidants and gets better as it ages. Just remember that and you'll feel less guilty.
24. **Dram I Am**: Flavorings in a dram? You need to know that a dram is a measurement equal to 1 teaspoon.
25. **Ignore The Fridge**: Cool candy slowly at room temperature. Don't be tempted to speed it by cooling in the refrigerator.
26. **Get Silly**: Sometimes the key to finding a new and delicious candy combination is trial and error. Chocolate with bacon ... yum. Candied jalapeños ... spicy yum!
27. **Heat It Up**: To keep melted chocolate warm longer after melting, place the bowl on an electric heating pad.
28. **Treats For A Year**: Make homemade fudge and caramel. These treats can be frozen and enjoyed for up to a year.
29. **Chocolate Creativity**: Don't toss out remaining dipping chocolate! Nuts, pretzels, raisins, marshmallows, cookies, and fruits can all be dipped for a candy-like snack.

Cookies

1. **Take A Chill**: Chill your cookie dough before baking. Leaving cookie dough in the fridge overnight allows it to absorb liquids and results in a full, yummy cookie.
2. **Keep 'Em Apart**: Store different kinds of cookies in separate containers. Moist cookies will soften crispy ones.
3. **Chewy Or Crispy Cookies**: Like chewy or prefer crispy? Baking your cookies a little less results in chewier cookies. Baking a little longer makes them crispier.
4. **Melting Magic**: Want to know the magic secret to chewy cookies? First, melt your butter halfway in a just-warm oven. Then cool it to room temperature in the fridge before creaming with sugar.
5. **Cookie Cravings**: When making cookie dough, make an extra roll and freeze for later cravings. Roll it into a log shape, wrap tightly in wax paper, and store in a plastic zipper bag in the freezer.
6. **Picture Perfect**: When making chocolate chip cookies, set some of the chocolate morsels aside. Place a few of them on top of each cookie before baking for a beautiful presentation.
7. **Halloween Helps**: Got leftover Halloween candy? Chop chocolate candies or candy corn pieces to use in place of chocolate chips in cookies.
8. **Burned Batch**: When you burn the bottoms of a batch of cookies, don't throw them out. Use a cheese grater to scrape off the burned part. Spread chocolate frosting between two cookies to make chocolate cookie sandwiches.

Cooking with Kids

1. **Go Slowly**: With kids, expect cooking to take longer than it would take you alone. For young children, the experience is as important as the end result.
2. **Embrace The Mess**: Cooking with kids is messy. Lay a vinyl tablecloth or shower curtain on the floor beneath where you're working and have fun.
3. **Choose Wisely**: Pick a recipe the kids like, with age-appropriate steps. Make sure you have everything ready and handy ahead of time.
4. **Don't Starve**: If you're cooking your evening meal with kids, try to do some prep before they join you. This will help you get dinner on the table sooner.
5. **Nothing Fancy**: Put the kids washable or disposable clothing. They're going to get dirty, even with an apron!
6. **Hairy Habits**: Explain how hairs can fall in food while cooking, making a meal unappetizing. Have long hair pulled back, away from faces. Hats help too.
7. **Cleanliness Matters**: Make sure hands are washed before cooking and frequently throughout. Explain the need to wash between touching raw foods and other foods.
8. **Wash With Words**: Teach children that to clean hands adequately for cooking they should use soap and water. They should rub their hands together vigorously while singing the ABC's to make sure they scrub long enough before rinsing.
9. **Bad Bacteria**: Discuss foodborne bacteria and how children can protect themselves. Also, require them to use a clean spoon each time they taste to avoid spreading germs. And remind them that finger licking is not allowed until the end!
10. **Reading Recipes**: Have older children read the steps and gather what's needed. Discuss the steps and make a game plan of what needs to be done next.

11. **Picture Time**: Younger children will learn better with their senses. Explain what's cooking by show pictures as you go along to better engage with them.
12. **Moving On**: Cooking is good for improving fine motor skills. Stirring, cutting, and decorating also help with hand-eye coordination.
13. **Learn As You Cook**: Discuss the ingredients you are using, where they come from, and how they are prepared. Different aspects of cooking can enhance so many learning opportunities.
14. **Tasty Tasting**: Encourage tasting as they cook. It makes for a more educational and enjoyable experience and encourages them to try new things.
15. **Age Ratings**: You may see recipes that have recommended age guidelines. Know your own child's abilities and what they are capable of and enjoy doing.
16. **Just Relax**: If you're stressed, your kids will find cooking less pleasant. If you are relaxed, your kids will learn to love cooking. If you're not an experienced cook, start with easy recipes and you can learn together.
17. **Only The Best**: Buy the best in-season fruits and veggies possible. Discuss what is available during different seasons where you live and why it's best to buy locally and organically when possible. Get your children to appreciate fruits and veggies at a young age.
18. **Embrace The Dirt**: Seeing the dirt on fruits and veggies tells kids where their food came from. Discuss the growing and harvesting process. If there is a farm in your area, see if it's possible to pick some produce yourselves. Explain how to clean the produce before using or eating.
19. **Rolling On**: One of the most fun baking activities for kids is using the rolling pin. Let them roll out cookies and crusts. It's a great way to work off pent-up energy!

20. **Meat Decisions**: Eating meat or going vegetarian/vegan is a personal choice. Help educate your children so they can make their own choice one day. The beef was once a mooing cow. The bacon came from an oinking pig.
21. **Know When To Say When**: Cooking is fun, but know when they've had enough. When they get bored and whine, you'll get upset and the fun experience will be over. Know when to let them stop participating.
22. **Learning From Cooking**: Use cooking as an experience to improve learning skills. Reading, science, and arithmetic are all parts of cooking. Don't waste the opportunity.
23. **Delicioso:** Cooking and eating foods from other countries and cultures is a great way to learn more about the world. Learning new culinary words improves vocabulary skills. Bon appétit!
24. **Nutrition Needs**: Children's diets are often lacking in essential nutrients due to over-processed convenience foods. Discuss the health benefits from eating freshly prepared meals. If they make the food, they'll be more apt to try it too.
25. **Junk The Junk**: If you have kids, don't stock your kitchen with junk food. Out of sight, out of mind. Buy delicious but healthy snacks for them and yourself.
26. **Bonding Time**: Use the process of preparing a meal to bond and build a relationship with your child. Cooking together requires teamwork and sharing and creates good memories to last a lifetime.

Crock Pots & Slow Cookers

1. **Simple Cleaning**: One of the best things about slow cookers is the easy cleanup. Because moisture is retained easily, scorching should be minimal. If your pot is hard to clean, it may have been on high heat too long.
2. **Experience Teaches**: Each slow cooker is different. Adjust times as needed to ensure proper cooking times and moisture levels.
3. **Cook And Freeze**: Don't cook a smaller portion of a recipe in your crockpot or the heating will not be correct. Make the whole recipe and freeze for meals another day.
4. **Fabulously Full**: When cooking with a crockpot, for best results don't over-fill or under-fill. Filling the pot about 1/2 – 3/4 full is the proper amount.
5. **Limit Liquids**: Cooking with a crockpot retains a lot of moisture. Practice with your recipes to see if you need to reduce the amount of liquid required in a crockpot.
6. **No Peeking**: Opening the lid for a stir or peek adds almost 15 to 20 minutes to needed cooking time. Leave it alone and let it cook.
7. **Ice Advice**: Don't add frozen or very cold food to your slow cooker. The addition can lead to an unsafe cooking temperature.
8. **Watch The Wine**: If you're adding wine as a flavoring, be careful not to use too much. The alcohol will not evaporate as much as in a high-heat pan on the stovetop.
9. **Power Problems**: Did the power go out while you were gone or did you forget to turn the pot on? Throw the food out and start again. The extra time it takes will be better for your health - don't risk getting food poisoning.
10. **Stay Cool**: Using a slow cooker in the summertime is a great way to keep the house cool. It's also an alternative to grilling when you don't feel like cooking over the heat outside.

11. **Thicken Up**: If the sauce or soup in your slow cooker is too liquid, take the lid off for the last 30 minutes of cooking. Some of the liquid will evaporate, making the sauce/soup thicker. Keep an eye on it to make sure only a small amount evaporates.

12. **Seafood Sensitivity**: Seafood doesn't like to cook in a slow cooker. Delicate seafood like shrimp should be added in the last hour of cooking to keep it from becoming rubbery.

13. **Healthy Slow Cooking**: Some studies have shown that long and steady temperature cooking is healthier. Fast, high-heat cooking may contribute to heart disease, cancer and diabetes. Embrace the benefits of the slow cooker!

14. **Layer In Order**: Recipes give a certain order in which ingredients should be combined. It's imperative that you layer ingredients in a crockpot in the order provided by the recipe.

15. **Cool It**: Bring your crockpot to room temperature before washing. Cold water on a hot pot could cause it to crack.

16. **Hot You Got**: Older crockpots usually cook at lower temperatures. Due to public demand, newer models cook at higher temperatures. Make sure you know your temps when replacing an older model.

17. **Bit Of Burn**: If your stew scorches a bit on the bottom of the slow cooker, don't panic. Stir in a little milk to help reduce the burn taste.

18. **Where's The Beef**: Choosing the right cut of beef is important for a crockpot. For best results, use stew beef, short ribs, or brisket instead of sirloin.

19. **Mix It Up**: The beauty of one-pot cooking is that you can combine many nutritional needs in one pot. Combine your veggies, meat, starch, and dairy with seasonings and cook all at once.

20. **Cheaper Meats**: By cooking at low heat, you can use less expensive, yet flavorful cuts of meat.

21. **Brown Before**: Slow cookers don't brown the meat you put inside. If you want your meat browned for your dish, do it before adding it to the slow cooker.
22. **Doing Rice Right**: Add your rice to your crockpot when it's set to high and 2 hours remain to cook. If your crockpot is cooking on the low setting, add the rice when 2 hours and 45 minutes are left to cook
23. **Dump Dessert**: Learn the secret of "dump cakes." With just a few simple ingredients like prepared cake mix, canned fruit, and butter, you can have a delicious and easy dessert in about 40 minutes.
24. **Rice Is Nice**: Use your crockpot as a rice cooker. Spray the inside with a non-stick spray. Add the usual 2:1 ratio of water to rice. When cooking brown rice, increase water by 1/2 cup. Cook on high for 2 hours.

Dips

1. **Minty Pea Dip**: Peas in dip? Yep, try this snack dip recipe - mash 1/2 cup thawed frozen peas with 1 tablespoon of minced mint and 2 teaspoon freshly squeezed lime juice. It's delicious with whole-wheat pretzels!
2. **Delicious Dips**: Prepare dips a couple of days ahead. It saves time and allows the flavors of the seasonings to blend together nicely.
3. **Fresh Guacamole**: Guacamole is delicious and avocados provide a helping of healthy oils. Store prepared guacamole in tightly sealed zipper bags (with the air pressed out) to delay browning.

Eggs

1. **Pan Preference**: When cooking fried eggs, any size pan will work. Try to match the number of eggs you're cooking to the pan size when possible.
2. **Timing The Top**: Getting a perfectly cooked fried egg top is tricky. To cook the whites but keep the yolks a little runny, cover the pan mid-cooking to trap heat and steam the tops.
3. **Hard-Boiled Or Raw**: Have trouble telling boiled eggs from raw in the fridge? Hold them up to a light. If any light is visible through the egg, it's raw.
4. **Fluffier Beaten Eggs**: Need the fluffiest beaten eggs? Bring the eggs to room temperature before beating.
5. **Fresh Or Old Eggs**: Remember that fresh eggshells appear rough and chalky. Older eggs will have a smoother and shinier appearance.
6. **Easy-Peel Eggshells:** When hard-boiling eggs, add two tablespoons of baking soda to the water. This changes the pH of the water, which results in eggshells that peel off more easily.

Fish & Seafood

1. **Fishy Business**: Ten minutes per inch for the thickest part of the fish is a good estimated cooking time.
2. **Bye Bye Fishy Taste**: When thawing frozen fish, place it in milk. Milk reduces the frozen, fishy taste and even makes it taste fresher.
3. **Flip Fish**: When cooking fish, don't move it around too much. You only need to cook one side, flip, and cook the other side. Done.
4. **Shrimp In A Hurry**: Buy frozen shrimp in bags and keep in freezer until needed. They can be easily thawed in a bowl in the fridge, or quicker by running cool water over them. There are endless recipes that call for shrimp, so always be prepared!

Frostings

1. **Trapped Crumbs**: For prettier cake frosting, first apply a thin coat of icing to the cake to trap the crumbs. Place the cake in the refrigerator for about 30 minutes to chill and then frost with a second layer.
2. **Fondant Flavor**: Fondant is the smooth frosting coating used on many wedding cakes. It looks pretty, but consists of gelatin, glycerin, and sugar, so it isn't as tasty as regular frosting.
3. **Two Tastes**: Can't decide between 2 tempting frosting flavors? On a layer cake, use both - spread one frosting between the 2 layers and the other on the sides and top.
4. **Colored Coconut**: Shredded coconut is another alternative, or addition, to frosting. To make colored coconut, place in a clean jar, add a few drops of food coloring, cap and shake until blended.
5. **Sprinkled Sugar**: No time to frost the cake? Sprinkle powdered sugar on top for a pretty look and sweet taste.
6. **Flower Power**: Look for beautiful edible flowers to top your cakes and desserts. A sprinkling of edible glitter makes them even more beautiful.
7. **Easy Breezy Frosting**: Easily make maple syrup frosting for autumn cakes. Simply combine maple syrup with powdered sugar until it reaches a frosting consistency.
8. **Satiny Smooth**: To make a smooth finish after frosting your cake, dip your knife in hot water. Next, run it along the top and sides to give your cake a perfectly smooth look.
9. **Frosting Substitute**: Use marshmallows instead. The marshmallows melts into a sweet, gooey frosting substitute.
10. **Frosting Fixes**: Want extra color and interesting flavors in your frosting? Stir a little bit of flavored, packaged gelatin mix into your store-bought frosting to make it special.

11. **Lace Stencil**: Instead of making a stencil for a powdered sugar cake topping, try using a piece of lace. Lay the lace fabric over the cake (or cupcake) and sprinkle powdered sugar on top. It will fall through the holes and leave the lacy pattern. A paper doily works, too.

12. **Frozen Frosted Cakes**: When you need to freeze a frosted cake, use buttercream frosting. Cooked and boiled icings do not freeze as well.

Frozen Treats

1. **Deter The Drip**: When eating sugar ice cream cones, drips can leak out and make a mess. Place a miniature marshmallow in the bottom of the sugar cone to stop drips (yum).
2. **Soft Serve**: Store your ice cream in a large zipper plastic bag in the freezer. This helps it stay softer so you can serve it more easily.
3. **Stop The Drips**: Paper muffin cups make great Popsicle drip-catchers. Push the Popsicle stick through the paper and slide up to the base of it.
4. **No Freezer Burn**: Press a piece of waxed paper onto the top of your ice cream surface. This will help deter ice crystals from forming on the ice cream.

Fruit

1. **Perfect Pineapple**: Trying to pick a perfectly ripe pineapple can be tricky. To test ripeness, pull a couple of leaves out (and a little up), not sideways. If they come out easily, it's ripe. A strong sweet smell can indicate over-ripeness.
2. **Blackberry Benefits**: Blackberries are a delicious addition to pastries and breakfast foods. A study from the University of Ohio determined that blackberries are one of the strongest cancer-fighting berries by almost 40%.
3. **Wash Later**: When purchasing blackberries, don't wash them until you are ready to use or freeze them. Washing them too soon can lead to spoiling and mold growth.
4. **Salty Citrus**: Grapefruit is naturally tangy and many people add sugar to sweeten it. Try adding a little salt, as it can intensify the sweetness as well.
5. **Boil Then Peel**: Scalding most fruits and vegetables before peeling will help make the job easier. Potatoes, tomatoes, and peaches are easily peeled this way.
6. **Keep The Pit**: If you need only half of an avocado, keep the other half with the pit. This will help keep it from browning as fast.
7. **Ripening Rate**: Increase the speed that fruits and vegetables ripen by placing them in a paper bag for a few days. Natural gasses will build up and ripen them faster.
8. **Stem Solution**: Press a plastic straw up through the bottom of a strawberry to remove the stem easily and neatly.
9. **More Juice Please**: To get more juice from a lemon or lime, roll it on the counter first, pressing down with the palm of your hand.
10. **Citrus Saver**: Freeze lemons and limes before they go to waste. Grate them for lemon and lime zest when needed.

Frying

1. **Perfect Point**: Deep-frying requires oil with a high smoke point (above 375°F) so the oil won't break down at the high temperature. Oils with appropriate high smoke points include peanut, canola, sunflower, and safflower.

2. **Eternal Enemies**: Water and oil don't mix. Adding water to hot oil can result in an explosion. Keep your fry area clean and dry and never store water nearby.

3. **Salt Splatters**: Salt food after frying to avoid splattering. Otherwise the salt will draw moisture to the surface of the cooking food, and can cause the hot oil to splatter.

4. **Avoid Plumbing Issues**: After frying, allow oil to cool completely for about 2 hours.   To avoid plumbing clogs, never pour the oil down the drain.

5. **Extinguisher Education**: Every kitchen needs an appropriate type of fire extinguisher, especially if frying. Learn the proper way to use it before an emergency arises.

6. **3 Rules To Success**: Don't overcrowd your frying pan. Don't allow coated food to sit for long periods of time. Turn the food once while it cooks, not over and over.

7. **Get Crumby**: When frying with bread crumbs, coat the food in flour first, next dip quickly in beaten egg, and finally coat with bread crumbs. The egg sticks to the flour and the crumbs stick to the egg.

8. **Avoid Springy Tongs**: Spring-loaded tongs aren't safe for frying. If your fingers slip, you might get burned by the oil or make a mess of your kitchen.

9. **Fight the Flames**: A range with a metal hood is safest when it comes to frying. If a fire occurs, flames from can shoot 2 to 3 feet in the air, catching shelves on fire.

10. **Tight And Thick**: When frying, choose tight-fitting, thick, long-sleeved clothing. This will prevent burns from splattering hot oil.

11. **Small Selections**: Small pieces fry better at higher temperatures. You'll achieve a crispier, less greasy result.
12. **Crazy Cooling**: Add pieces to your fryer separately. Adding too much at once cools the oil quickly.
13. **Know When To Throw**: You can reuse fryer oil but change it when it becomes dark. Not doing so will make foods taste the same and can cause a rancid taste.
14. **Paper Pats**: When removing food from the fryer, allow excess oil to drip back into the pan. Spread food on a paper towel on a plate to absorb remaining oil.
15. **Fat Fables**: Pan-frying food is not necessarily unhealthy. When it's done properly, very little oil is actually absorbed and eaten.
16. **Foaming Fails**: Oil foam happens when oil breaks down due to high heat and overuse. Foaming oil should not be used; discard properly.
17. **Temp Tricks**: Heat oil to the proper temperature. If it's too hot, it will burn the coating before the food is cooked on the inside. If it's too cool, it will soak in and make foods soggy and oily. Use a cooking thermometer.
18. **Best Bacon**: Bacon likes lower heats for pan-frying. Cooking at a lower heat will lessen shrinking, burning and curled edges.
19. **Bacon Bites**: Don't fry whole slices of bacon for crumbling. Chop or cut raw bacon into small pieces and cook until crispy. No nibbling!
20. **Dunk And Cover**: Dunk chicken in buttermilk with salt and pepper, then cover in seasoned all-purpose flour. This will help make a light, crispy outside for fried chicken.
21. **Be Cool**: Give fried chicken a chance to rest and cool down. Immediately after frying, it's terribly hot and can cause burns.

22. **Go Deep**: Cooking in a cast iron pan makes delicious fried chicken. Select a deep pan that will hold enough oil to cook the chicken completely and safely.

23. **Turning Time**: Not sure when it's time to turn your fried food? Food should be turned when it lifts easily from the pan. If it's sticking, it's not ready to flip.

24. **Burn-Free Butter**: When using whole butter for pan-frying and sautéing, use a moderate, not high, heat. Butter has a low smoke and burn point.

25. **Cord Caution**: Never use an extension cord when using an electric deep fryer. Extension cords are made short intentionally to avoid the dangers of having a hot oil spill.

26. **Frying The Bird**: Fried turkey is delicious for Thanksgiving. Be sure the turkey is fully thawed before placing in oil. If you're really feeling adventurous, wrap the entire turkey with bacon strips before frying.

27. **Keeping It Warm**: If you can't eat fried food right away, place it in a 200-degree oven. This will keep it crisp and at a safe temperature to eat later.

28. **Fried Goodness**: For a delicious treat, deep-fry mini candy bars dipped in funnel cake batter. Freeze candy bars first, dip in batter, place in oil, and turn once.

29. **Splatter Saving**: Don't have a splatter screen when frying? In a pinch, make one out of a disposable aluminum pie pan. Poke holes in the pan and place upside down over frying food to block the pops and splatters.

Grilling

1. **Gas Or Charcoal:** It's a preference mainly. Gas burns cleaner. Charcoal gives off more carbon monoxide and other pollutants, but gives a more classic barbecue flavor.
2. **Just Add Water:** Grilling with fatty meats can lead to flare-ups. Keep a small spray bottle of water nearby to tame the flames.
3. **Direct And Indirect Heat:** When grilling a food that takes less than 20 minutes to cook, direct heat is best. If a food takes more than 20 minutes, use indirect heat.
4. **Best Bamboo:** For a timesaver, soak a bunch of bamboo skewers for an hour and then freeze them in a zipper plastic bag. When needed, pull them out of the freezer to use pre-soaked. The water will help prevent the skewers from burning on the grill.
5. **Charcoal Conditions:** Light charcoal 30 minutes before needed for cooking. Make sure the flame has gone down and charcoal is ashy-gray before placing meat on the grill.
6. **No Wires:** Clean your grill with a crumpled-up piece of aluminum foil. Wire bristles can come off brushes and get into foods.
7. **Safe Start:** Always light your gas grill with the lid up. Lighting it closed may cause gas to build up inside.
8. **Stop The Fire:** Consider using ceramic briquettes. They do not catch on fire like lava briquettes do.
9. **Lighter Fluid Only:** When lighting a charcoal grill, never use gasoline or kerosene. To ensure maximum safety, use only charcoal lighter fluid.
10. **Preheat Properly:** Just like an oven, you should preheat your grill to get a good sear. Get the heat going about 10-15 minutes before placing food on the grill.
11. **Plenty of Propane:** Always keep a full bottle of propane in storage. Running out mid-barbecue will spoil the fun and the food.

12. **Hold the Bacteria**: Refrigerate grilled leftovers as soon as possible. Leaving leftovers out for more than an hour may make them unsafe to eat.
13. **Germ Buster**: Don't reuse a plate that has held raw meat until it's been washed. You can contaminate other foods with dangerous bacteria.
14. **Honor Thy Thigh**: Chicken thighs are one of the best grill choices. They have a stronger chicken flavor than breast pieces and can withstand the heat of the grill.
15. **No Stick**: Foods can stick when placed directly on the grill rack. Reduce the problem by oiling the rack (before heating) with a paper towel soaked in vegetable oil.
16. **Fatty = Flavor**: When grilling burgers, don't go lean. An 80/20 blend will give you the right fat balance for the perfect, juicy burger.
17. **Butcher Buddies**: Your butcher can give you the best cuts for your grill. Steer clear of the moisture-filled, preservative soaked, plastic-packaged steaks.
18. **Fish Feast**: Always thaw frozen seafood before cooking it. Place fillets in an oiled grill basket. Fish steaks and whole fish go directly on the greased grill, and scallops and shrimp go on bamboo skewers.
19. **Stick-Free**: Keep grilled fish from sticking to the hot grill. Lay a bed of sliced lemons directly on the grill and place fish on top.
20. **Tennis Balls**: A good way to judge how big a hamburger patty should be is to think of a tennis ball. Form a ball of hamburger that size before flattening it into a patty.
21. **The Perfect Shape**: To keep the burger shape, make a nickel-sized, 1/4-inch deep indentation with your thumb in the center of the patty. This stops the burger from becoming a rounded ball and keeps it flat.
22. **No Squishing**: Flattening a burger with a spatula while grilling presses the juices out. Instead, use the thumb indention technique to keep burgers flat.

23. **Grill That Bird**: You can grill a turkey in your barbecue pit. Make sure the bird fits and the door will close. A 12-pound turkey works best.

24. **Defrost First**: Don't grill a frozen turkey, as it will cook unevenly. It will be almost impossible to tell which parts have fully cooked enough to be safe to eat.

25. **Beautiful Buns**: To add to the beauty of your perfect burger, make sure to choose the perfect bun. Experiment with different types of rolls to find your favorite combination ... French rolls, onion rolls, pretzel buns etc.

26. **Warm Storage**: To keep hamburgers warm after removing from the grill, store in a tortilla warmer. It keeps the food warm and is easy to transport.

27. **Burned Sauce**: When grilling, wait to add sauce until during the last 10-15 minutes of cooking. Adding sauce at the beginning will cause the sugars to burn on the food.

28. **Don't Lose The Marbles**: For best flavor, look for thin streaks of fat in the steak. That's the "marbling" that adds juiciness and flavor.

29. **Choosing The Cut**: When selecting pre-packaged steaks, watch out for excess liquid in the packaging tray. This may be a result of previous freezing and thawing, or too much time in the meat case.

30. **Know When To Stop**: Undercooking a steak is better than overcooking. You can't un-cook an overdone piece of meat, but you can cook a rare piece more.

31. **Bigger Means Slower**: When cooking a larger cut of meat, cook it slowly at a lower heat. This will result in a more tender and juicy meat.

32. **Wait On It**: Don't add salt to liquid marinade. Salt the meat just prior to grilling to avoid throwing it out with the excess marinade.

33. **Pass The Wine**: Red wine contains natural anti-oxidants. But did you know that marinating beef in red wine for six hours prior to grilling reduces carcinogens that form during the cooking process? Viva la vino!

34. **Stainless Steel Success**: When mixing acidic marinades, use a stainless steel bowl. Stainless steel does not react with acids.
35. **Take It Easy**: When applying rubs, don't press too hard. Rubbing hard can damage meat fibers and result in over-seasoning.
36. **Onions Have Layers**: To grill chunky onions without them falling apart, place large pieces on skewers. Place on grill until roasted and tender.
37. **Freshly Ironed Sandwich**: You can make a grilled cheese sandwich using an iron just like you see in the movies. Butter the outside of the bread, insert cheese between slices, and wrap it in heavy foil. Put your iron on the high setting (no steam) and iron for about 5 minutes on each side.

Healthy Cooking

1. **Grainy Goodness**: Boost the fiber in your snacks by sticking with whole grain. You can find whole grain pretzels, tortillas, breads and cereals.

2. **Specialty Snacks**: Offer healthy snacks you and your family have never tried before. Avocado slices, seaweed chips, rice cakes, dried cranberries, jicama, goji berries and star fruit are choices worth trying.

3. **Delicious Distraction**: If you have a habit of grazing while you cook, chew gum while cooking. You'll save calories by laying off the extras.

4. **Fiber Is Fabulous**: A lack of fiber in your diet can lead to many health problems. To add daily fiber to your diet, prepare a salad packed with veggies and healthy grains for lunch.

5. **Fight The Fat**: Store canned broth in the refrigerator to cause the fat to solidify. When ready to use, punch 2 small holes on each end of the can top. When you pour the broth into a recipe, the fat will stay in the can.

6. **Wild Thing**: Wild rice is delicious and adds fiber to your meals. Cook wild rice until it expands and you can see the lighter portion of the interior grain. Don't overcook.

7. **Meal Geometry**: Here's a simple meal math tip. For a nutritious meal, your veggies should take up 1/2 of the plate. Your meat and grain/starch should each take up 1/4 of the plate.

Dairy: What's Healthy?

1. **Basic Butter Is Better**: Unless your recipe specifically calls for salted butter, choose unsalted. You can always add salt to your recipe if needed.
2. **Stop The Stick**: Margarines and shortenings are thick because of the types of oil they're made of. Try to use more heart-healthy vegetables oils instead.
3. **Cheesy Cheats**: Cheese can contain quite a bit of salt. When your recipe calls for cheese, try to use fresh mozzarella or low sodium cheeses.
4. **Dairy Dilemma**: Dairy products such as cheese are naturally high in fat and not as heart healthy. Look for reduced-fat choices such as feta and skim mozzarella.
5. **Monitor Milk**: Most people can't tell the difference between whole milk and reduced-fat milk, especially in cooking. Choose reduced-fat over whole as a more heart-healthy option.
6. **Baby Steps**: Once you've gotten used to the taste and texture of reduced-fat products, continue the switch to fat-free. By taking it in steps, you're more likely to accept the change in taste.

Healthy Oils, Fats and Proteins

1. **Smart Sauté:** When using this cooking method, choose heart-healthy oil. Only use small amounts of canola, olive, or soybean oils when sautéing.
2. **Super Salads:** Don't turn a healthy salad choice into an unhealthy one by dousing it with fatty dressing. Make your own salad dressings using small amounts of olive, walnut, or pecan oil with lemon juice, salt and pepper.
3. **Omega-3 Benefits:** Research has shown that omega-3 fatty acids are a healthy part of your diet. When choosing oils, look for those that contain omega-3 fatty acids, such as canola, soybean, and flaxseed oil.
4. **Fresh Flax:** Use omega-3-rich flaxseed oil fresh from the bottle in salads or as a tasty alternative to butter on cooked vegetables. Refrigeration keeps it tasting fresh.
5. **Slow the Spray:** When possible, avoid using oil spray. It adds more calories and fat than you'd think. If baking, parchment paper is a healthier choice.
6. **Trans Fat Trap:** Many processed baked goods are high in unhealthy oils and trans-fat. Read the labels or bake fresh at home to ensure healthiness.
7. **Want Walnuts:** Walnuts are an excellent way to add a heart-healthy punch to your everyday foods. Chopped walnuts are delicious added to cereal, oatmeal, salads and muffins. They're high in calories, so eat them in small amounts.
8. **Super Eggs:** Some, but not all, chickens are raised given high omega-3 feed. This results in a higher omega-3 egg. All eggs do contain cholesterol, so even these more heart-healthy eggs should be limited.

Kick Up the Flavor!

1. **Pungent Punches**: Using garlic and onions will jumpstart the other flavors in your recipe. Whether added raw or cooked in a healthy oil, they add a delicious twist to your food.
2. **Hot, Hot, Hot:** Jalapeños and other hot peppers provide an explosion of flavor and heat. Add these powerful spices to chili, tacos, and salsa instead of so much salt. Remove the seeds to lessen the hotness.
3. **All About That Base**: To build up the flavor in your meal, used simmered meat stocks. Add wine and herbs to make a flavorful sauce.

Pick Your Meats Carefully

1. **Lean And Light**: When choosing meat, look for leaner beef and pork. If the words "loin" or "round" are in the name, it's a healthier choice.
2. **Time For A Trim**: Fat and skin add flavor to cooking but aren't healthy for your heart. Do yourself a favor by trimming off the fat and removing the skin. You'll barely notice the difference, but your heart will!
3. **Go Light On Lunchmeat**: Hot dogs, bologna, salami, sausage, and bacon are not heart-healthy foods. Look for substitutes made with turkey when possible and try to avoid processed deli meat altogether.
4. **Favorite Fish**: Fish is a naturally heart-healthy food. Eat it frequently using different low-oil cooking methods such as baking, broiling, and grilling.
5. **Fish Facts**: Fatty fish contains the "good" oils. Try to include some in your meals each week by selecting salmon, albacore tuna, and sardines.
6. **Tasty Tuna**: Choose water-packed tuna in cans instead of oil-packed. The calories are almost a third less with water.
7. **Veggie Variety**: You don't always have to eat meat to get protein. Choose plant foods such as soybeans, beans, nuts and lentils occasionally, and get the protein and fiber with less fat.

Preparation Matters

1. **Preparation Pointer**: Use cooking methods that use less oil. Baking, broiling, grilling, and roasting are great ways to prepare meats without a lot of additional fat.
2. **Scoop The Stew**: Refrigerate stews and soups overnight. When you're ready to reheat, skim the fat off with a spoon first.
3. **Diligently Drain**: When preparing ground beef, always drain any excess fat off after cooking. The greasy fat that hardens when it cools doesn't need to end up in your body.

Salt Smarts

1. **Health Trumps Convenience**: Avoid packaged convenience foods because they often have salt as a preservative. Cook for yourself so you know how much salt has been added.
2. **Salty Sides**: Make homemade brown rice or baked potatoes instead of the packaged instant potatoes or flavored rice/noodles. The salt content in these is way over the recommended daily allowance.
3. **Read The Label**: Always read the food label for sodium. Watch for alternate products that say "sodium-free," "low sodium," or "no salt."
4. **Salty Seasonings**: Use salty seasonings such as broth, soy sauce, bouillon, seasoned salts, and condiments sparingly. They are all produced to be very high in salt.
5. **Control The Salt**: Remember you can always add more salt. There is no great way to take it back out.
6. **Additive Advice**: MSG, baking soda, and baking powder all include sodium. You may not be able to cut these out altogether, but be careful of adding additional salt to products that contain them.
7. **Trade Time**: If a recipe calls for salt, choose something healthier. Try spices such as rosemary, thyme, tarragon, onion and garlic powder, pepper, and even combinations. If you don't trust your novice taste buds, sprinkle in a salt-free seasoning from the store.
8. **Crazy Canning**: Salt is often added to canned vegetables. Go healthier by using only fresh, frozen, or salt-free canned veggies.
9. **Rinse The Veggies**: If you can't find low- or no-salt canned veggies, drain and rinse them before cooking. This will remove a large portion of the salt.
10. **Magical Marinades**: Rather than using salty condiments to marinate meat before grilling, try a citrus juice. Orange and

pineapple juice can be used as a delicious base for a meat marinade.

11. **Make The Break**: Out of sight, out of mind. The best way to cut down on salt is to not have it stocked in your kitchen.

12. **Low Fat, High Sodium**: Foods labeled as low fat can have high sodium content. The trade-off of fat and calories may mean too much salt in your diet. Read labels carefully!

13. **Super Seaweed**: When cooking beans, add a bit of dried seaweed (kombu or wakame) as a substitute for salt. It adds a delicious salty flavor that is lower in sodium and higher in iodine.

14. **Frozen Frequency**: When looking for frozen dinners, watch out for high sodium. Choose those that have 600 milligrams of sodium per serving or less. Restrict yourself to only one frozen entree daily.

Meats

1. **Mash Your Hamburger**: Need finely separated hamburger bits rather than chunks? Use a potato masher to make fine pieces when browning hamburger.
2. **Browned Meat**: Meat browns more easily when dry. Blot with a paper towel before adding to hot oil.
3. **Bonus With Bones**: Cooking with the bones left in makes meat cook a bit faster. The bones hold in the heat and distribute it more evenly throughout the meat.
4. **Let It Rest**: Meat continues cooking when you take it off the heat. Allow it to rest and seal in the juices before cutting and eating.
5. **Broth Cubes**: Chicken and beef broth usually comes in large containers, so there is usually some left over. Freeze the extra broth in ice cube trays to toss into future recipes.
6. **Best Burgers**: When making meatballs or patties, mix your meat and seasonings first. Then make a small patty to cook and taste before making the batch. Adjust seasonings as needed.
7. **Temperature Test**: Check the temperature of meats with a meat thermometer instead of cutting with a knife. The thermometer better gauges doneness and juices don't run out.
8. **Save The Bacon**: Cut the new bacon package in half and store in a zipper plastic bag. The size is better for cooking and easier to store.
9. **Pale Gravy**: Add just a few grains of instant coffee to the gravy. This adds a rich color without changing the taste
10. **Tender Touch:** For tender, juicy chicken breasts, soak them in buttermilk in the fridge for 3-4 hours before breading and frying.

Microwave Cooking

1. **It's Got The Power:** Each microwave oven is a little different. Learn your microwave's cooking power and adjust your cooking times and power levels accordingly. Blindly following the cooking times on the food packaging may result in a poorly cooked item.
2. **Safety First:** When cooking in the microwave, make sure you use dishes that are "microwave safe." Some materials can't take the heat and may melt. Metals will make sparks.
3. **Down With Damage:** If your microwave oven shows signs of damage, such as a cracked or poorly sealing door, it's time to replace it. The door protects you from the radiation.
4. **Outside First:** Remember that microwaves cook the outside of food first. Even if your food feels warm, make sure it's cooked all the way through for safety.
5. **Defrost Fact:** If you use your microwave to defrost food, don't keep it in so long that the food starts cooking. A 1lb steak should be defrosted for only about 6-9 minutes at most (check frequently).
6. **Vital Vitamins:** Microwave cooking has a bad reputation for destroying nutrients. Not true! Microwaves cook food quickly, preserving more nutrients.
7. **Round And Round:** If your microwave does not come with a carousel, be sure to turn your container every few minutes. The rotation helps ensure more even cooking.
8. **Don't Be A Square:** Don't use square cooking containers in the microwave. The foods tend to cook unevenly in the corners.
9. **Metal Madness:** When it comes to metals, some are microwave safe and others are quite dangerous. Unless your microwave recipe or product specifically calls for using a small amount of aluminum foil, avoid metals completely.
10. **Cover Up:** Covering microwave dishes helps food cook faster by steaming it and keeping it moist. Remove covers carefully to avoid steam burns.

11. **Pottery Problems:** If you are microwaving in pottery and the food isn't cooking well, the glaze may be the problem. Containers made with metallic glazes may block out the microwaves.

12. **Melamine Mistake:** Melamine is a common substance used to make plates and bowls. However, the plastic-like chemical gets hot and softens in the microwave. It's not microwave-safe.

13. **Pitch The Package:** Microwaves can be useful for defrosting frozen meat. However, never defrost in the store packaging; it's not made for the heat of microwaves.

14. **Bad For Babies:** Don't warm baby bottles in the microwave. The microwave method may make the bottle seem cool on the outside, but it may have hot spots inside.

15. **Put A Ring On It:** When cooking in the microwave, arrange individual foods like potatoes in a ring formation. This will help the food cook more uniformly throughout.

16. **Easy Cleanup:** Heat a bowl of water in the microwave on high for several minutes. The water will steam which helps messes wipe off easily.

17. **Ice Cream Issues:** Need softer ice cream for desserts? Remove ice cream from its tub onto a plate or bowl and microwave for 10-second intervals on high power. No more bent spoons!

18. **Caution With Water:** Water can be heated to boiling quickly in the microwave. Use caution! Microwave-boiled water may not bubble, but can still cause serious burns or a superheated explosion.

19. **Popping Poultry:** If your chicken makes loud popping sounds when heating in the microwave, pierce the skin. Piercing allows the steam to escape, reducing the pops.

20. **Chewy Toppings:** Add cheeses and other toppings at very end of microwave time. Adding them early will make them chewy, dried out, or soggy.

21. **Toasting In The Microwave:** Your microwave can be used to toast ingredients for baking. Shredded coconut, fresh

breadcrumbs, and nuts (minus shells) can all be toasted. Cook on high power at 1-minute intervals for up to 5 minutes as needed.

22. **Bacon Bits:** Make quick bacon bits in the microwave. Place bacon between paper towels on a microwave-safe plate. Cook on high for 1-minute intervals. Cook thoroughly, cool, and tear or cut into small bits.

23. **Quick Taters:** Potatoes can be baked quickly in the microwave. Wash and dry potatoes and pierce with a knife. Place on a paper towel on a plate and microwave on high for about 10 minutes. They will be very steamy; use caution to avoid burns. Test for doneness with a knife.

24. **Toothpick Taters**: Stick 3 or 4 toothpicks into each potato before microwaving. Standing on the toothpicks will promote quicker, more even cooking. Picture a table with toothpicks as the legs and the potato as the tabletop.

25. **Microwave Then Mash**: If you're mashing potatoes, microwave them instead of boiling. Since they're getting mashed, the cooking method doesn't matter and it saves time.

26. **No-Grill Corn On The Cob:** Place whole corncobs in microwave and cook on high for about 6 minutes. Let sit for about 5 minutes, remove the husks and silk, and top with butter.

27. **Soft Spread:** Use your microwave to soften butter to spread on bread. Place butter on a microwave-safe plate and warm it in 15-second intervals. Check for desired softness each time.

28. **Quick Sauce:** To make a quick and easy butter sauce for pasta, mix butter, pepper, lemon, and minced garlic together in a bowl. Microwave at 20-second intervals. Stir and check for desired liquidity.

29. **Homemade Applesauce:** Want fresh applesauce without lots of sugar? Combine 1 pound of peeled, diced apples with 1/4 cup water, 2 teaspoons sugar, and 1/8 teaspoon cinnamon in a large bowl. Cover and cook on high for about

8 to 10 minutes until soft. When done, mash with a fork and chill or serve warm.

Nuts & Seeds

1. **Go Nuts**: If your recipe needs ground nuts, be sure not to over-process them into nut butter. Put no more than 2 cups of nuts in your food processor and pulse at 3-second intervals. Check frequently to ensure you are getting the desired texture.
2. **Pumpkin Seed Perfection:** When using pumpkins, save the seeds for roasting. Rinse in a colander, toss with 2 teaspoons melted butter, spread on a baking sheet, then bake about 45 minutes at 300 degrees F until golden brown, stirring occasionally. Pumpkin seeds are rich in iron, magnesium, potassium, zinc, and iron.

Pastas

1. **Spoon Magic**: Water in pasta can often boil over, making a mess. Avoid this by placing a wooden spoon across the top of the pot. The wood doesn't absorb the moisture from the bubbles and actual repels it away. It's like magic! See for yourself.
2. **Easy Grains**: Cook a large batch of healthy grains, such as brown rice or quinoa, once a week to use for salads and sides during the week. Store in an airtight tub in the refrigerator.
3. **Perfect Pasta**: When making lasagna, make sure the filling and sauce is spread completely and thoroughly over the entire pasta. Missing areas can cause the pasta to dry out.
4. **Sticky Spaghetti**: To keep pasta from sticking together, use plenty of water (about 5 quarts per pound of dry pasta). Stir as soon as the pasta is added to the water to separate the noodles.
5. **Pasta Pairing**: When choosing pasta and sauce pairings, remember that thinner pastas pair best with thin sauces. Chunky pastas go best with chunky sauces. Thicker pastas, like fettuccine, go great thicker sauces. Easy to remember!
6. **A Little Pat**: Add a little pat of butter to spaghetti before boiling. This will reduce boiling over and sticking together.
7. **Spare A Minute**: Cook your pasta until one minute before time's up. Then drain and add to simmering sauce and let them cook the rest of the way. That way you don't overcook your pasta when combining with the sauce.
8. **Mac & Cheese Please**: When you make macaroni and cheese, use only one pan by not pre-cooking the pasta. Mix the dried pasta with a thinner, liquid milk/cheese sauce, and bake for about 30 minutes until tender and bubbly.

Pizza

1. **Pizza Perfection**: Does your pizza crust get soggy while baking? To help keep the crust crispy, try putting a layer of cheese on before and after the sauce.
2. **Pizza On The Pit**: Yes, you can grill pizza on the barbecue. If you want fresh grilled veggies on top, grill them first and add to the pizza as it cooks. Don't put raw veggies on the pizza as it cooks.
3. **Pizza Pointer**: Don't have a pizza cutter? Use kitchen scissors to cut the perfect size slices easily.

Planning Ahead

1. **Fill The Freezer**: If you want to buy in bulk for your freezer, know which items can stay frozen longest. Purchase whole chickens, bread, and fresh fruits and veggies to store in the freezer for up to 12 months.

Potatoes

1. **Vertical Spuds**: When baking many potatoes at one time, bake them standing on end in a muffin tin to save oven space. You'll have room in the oven for another dish.
2. **Quicker Sliced Potatoes**: Need cut potatoes for French fries in a hurry? Use an apple slicer to cut perfectly sized steak fries.
3. **Smooth Move**: The secret to smooth, lump-free mashed potatoes is to mash the cooked potatoes thoroughly before adding milk.

Salads

1. **Sanitary Salad**: When washing lettuce and greens, wash from the leaf end down to the stem. Naturally, most dirt will be on the soil end of the stem, and washing this way keeps dirt from washing onto the leaf.
2. **From Meat To Salad**: Have a hard time getting a meat-and-potato-lover to try salad? Make a hearty "steak salad" with strips of steak and cooked potatoes over lettuce and other salad veggies. Top with favorite dressing.
3. **Shake It Baby**: Stock up on mason jars for easy salad dressing preparation and storage. Just add ingredients, seal lid securely, and shake to blend thoroughly.
4. **Vinaigrette Value**: To make a simple, traditional vinaigrette, use 3 parts oil and 1 part vinegar. Add seasonings to taste.

Sautéing

1. **Large And Wide**: A skillet or sauté pan will work for sautéing. You just need a large surface to avoid overcrowding the food. Nonstick and stainless steel pans both work well for this cooking technique.
2. **Tender Time**: Sautéing means cooking time is short; this requires tender foods. Tough meats like brisket are best cooked long and with low heat.
3. **Small Bites**: Foods that are to be sautéed should be cut uniformly into bite-sized pieces. This will aid even cooking and avoid burning or toughness.
4. **Heat It Up**: Warm your sauté pan over medium heat for a few minutes before adding food and increase heat as needed. With heat that is too low, your foods will release juices and steam instead of sauté.
5. **Oil Is Second**: Get your pan hot first and then add the oil or butter, swirling to cover the pan bottom. Heat the fat for only about 10 to 30 seconds and then add the food.
6. **Strategically Stir**: Tender veggies and small meat pieces should be stirred often to brown and cook properly. Thick veggies such as potatoes should be stirred less frequently to keep them tender without falling apart.
7. **Stir-Frying Or Sautéing**: The cooking methods are similar as they both use fast cooking and small amounts of oils. However, stir-frying cooks food with higher heat and constant stirring.
8. **To Stick Or Not Stick:** Non-stick pans are fine for sautéing if you're not making a sauce from the pieces in the pan. Use a regular pan for making sauces.
9. **Listen For The Sizzle:** When you place your meat or veggie in the pan, you should hear a distinct sizzle. If you don't hear that sound, the pan is not hot enough.

10. **Mouthwatering Mushrooms**: To make the perfect mushrooms, place 8 ounces in a large pan in a single layer. Cook for 4-5 minutes in 2 tablespoons of butter until tender and light brown.
11. **Sparkling 'Shrooms**: Mushrooms change color when stir-fried. To add flavor and help retain some of the white color, add a few drops of lemon juice before cooking.
12. **Broth Or Butter**: Trying to reduce fat in your diet? Try doing a sauté using broth instead of butter or oil.
13. **No Brown Butter**: When sautéing vegetables like onions, combine equal portions of olive oil and butter. This will help keep the butter from browning.

Savvy Shopping

1. **Bulk Butter**: Buy butter in bulk when it's on sale so you'll have plenty on hand for holiday baking. Freeze it in plastic zipper storage bags for up to 6 months.
2. **Seasonal Suggestions**: Buying produce while it's in season will taste fresher, adds variety, and is more budget friendly.
3. **Well-Stocked Pantry**: Be sure to keep your pantry and freezer stocked with handy ingredients that can be used for multiple quick dishes. Pasta, tomato sauce, salsa, rice, frozen or canned vegetables, and broth can be used in endless ways.
4. **Holiday Hurrying**: As the holidays approach, check your pantry early on. Stock up before the rush on essentials you know you'll need.

Snacks

1. **Popcorn Salt**: Use a spice grinder or food processor to grind salt to powder. The powder salt will stick to popcorn better, with less falling to the bottom of the bowl.
2. **Salt Early**: When popping popcorn in an air popper or on the stove top, add salt before the popping begins. The salt will be better dispersed and soak into the popcorn better than shaking on when done.
3. **Need The Nuts**: Nuts are a convenient, healthy snack that provide good fat and fiber. Store nuts in the freezer to keep them fresh longer.

Soups & Chili

1. **Let It Be**: When making soup, cook it a day ahead of when you want to serve it. The flavors will blend over time and be twice as delicious.
2. **Saving Spiciness**: If you make your chili too spicy, try adding a couple of teaspoons of honey. The sweetness should balance out the spiciness.
3. **Fooling The Fat**: To remove excess fat from refrigerated soup, lay a sheet waxed paper over the soup before refrigerating it. Once the soup cools, gently lift the waxed paper and fat away.

Spices, Seasonings & Sweeteners

1. **Hot As Fire**: Looking for a pepper to really spice up your chili? Try the tiny but mighty habanero. Be warned, it's seriously hot!

2. **Safe Snips**: To avoid getting too much hot pepper on your hands, hold a pepper by the stem and snip it with kitchen scissors directly into the recipe. Your hands won't touch the spicy flesh or seeds.

3. **Simple Syrup**: Make a simple syrup to sweeten tea easily. Mix 1 cup each of water and sugar and warm on the stove over medium heat, stirring until sugar is completely liquefied. Keep in the fridge for up to 2 weeks.

4. **Restore Your Honey**: If your honey has crystallized, place the container in very warm water for 5-10 minutes to bring it back to its liquid state. Repeat as needed.

5. **Slippery Seeds**: Need citrus juice? Lemons, limes, and oranges can be squeezed over a grater or sieve placed on a bowl. The juice flows into the bowl and the seeds stay out.

6. **Frozen Zest**: After juicing a citrus fruit, don't just toss it. Take the time to remove the zest with a grater. Save it in a small container in the freezer. Citrus zest adds an extra punch to many dishes.

7. **Stinky Hands**: Cooking with fresh garlic can leave your hands stinky. Stainless steel items like spoons will remove the smell if you rub them over your hands.

8. **Hold The Smell**: If you need crushed garlic, place it in a plastic bag first. Using the back of a knife, smash it inside the bag. The smell will not get into your cutting board.

9. **Chill Instead Of Chopping**: Keep parsley in the freezer in a zipper plastic bag. When needed, take it out and rub the bag briskly between your hands. The parsley will break apart.

10. **Small Spices**: Need to take spices along for camping or travel? Use empty TicTac containers to carry small portions that are easily dispensed.
11. **Fresh Herbs**: Grow or buy fresh herbs and freeze them in zipper plastic bags. They're far better tasting than dried bottled herbs from the store.
12. **Homemade Seasonings**: Stop buying the expensive seasoning packets at the store. To save money, look up seasoning combinations on the Internet, make them and store them in jars.

Substitution Secrets

1. **Not Exactly Egg**: Want a little extra nutrition in your muffins, breads, and cakes? Mix a teaspoon of flaxseed meal with 3 teaspoons of water. Substitute for 1 egg in your recipe.

2. **Hi Applesauce**: Unsweetened applesauce averages 80-100 calories per cup and has 2-3 grams of fiber. Trading out applesauce for sugar can help prevent weight gain. When substituting applesauce for granulated sugar, reduce the liquid in your original recipe by 2-3 tablespoons for each cup of applesauce.

3. **Milk + Acid = Curdle**: When using milk in an acidic recipe, your milk can easily curdle. Use whole milk to combat this.

4. **Cake To Cupcakes**: Have a cake recipe you want to use for cupcakes? An 8-inch layer cake recipe (2 layers) will make about 20-24 cupcakes.

5. **Oily Options**: You can trade some puréed fruits and veggies such as apples, bananas, pears, squash, and pumpkin for part of the oils in your recipes. If your recipe says 1 cup of oil, you can use 3/4 cup puréed fruit or veggies and 1/4 cup oil for a healthy substitution.

6. **In The Raw**: Raw sugar can be substituted for white sugar. However, the end result may be a slightly darker color for your baked good.

7. **Cuckoo For Coconut**: For a change of pace, try using coconut milk instead of whipped cream. Place a container of coconut milk in the refrigerator overnight then use a hand mixer and whip until it's creamy. Add sugar and vanilla if additional sweetness is desired.

8. **Powder Power**: Use confectioner's (powdered) sugar instead of granulated when making whipped cream. The results will be fluffier and longer lasting.

9. **Cracked Up**: When a recipe calls for cracker crumbs, breadcrumbs are interchangeable. One cup of breadcrumbs equals 3/4 cup of cracker crumbs.

Sugar

1. **Brick Sugar**: If your brown sugar has hardened into a brick, use a cheese-grater to grate off the amount you need. The remaining part can be softened with a slice of bread in the bag.
2. **Sugar Measurements**: One cup of granulated sugar is equal to 1-3/4 cups of confectioner's sugar. Do not substitute in baking.

Tacos

1. **Taco Shell Liners**: Place a whole lettuce leaf inside a taco shell and pile on the meat and cheese. This keeps the moisture off the shell and reduces cracking.
2. **Taco in Tines**: Use the tines of your fork to hold your taco shell upright on your plate while you add the toppings.
3. **Quick Shells**: To make quick and easy taco salad bowls from tortillas, use a muffin or cupcake pan. Flip the pan over, shape tortillas in the spaces between the cup holders and bake until crispy.

Tools of the Trade

1. **Spatula Smarts**: Tongs can tear and break delicate fish flesh. A spatula will help fish stay together better.
2. **Glass Or Metal**: You can bake cakes in glass or metal pans. However, when using glass, lower the oven temperature 25 degrees.
3. **Handle Helper**: If you have a metal pan lid, slide a couple of corks under the handle to help avoid burning your hand.
4. **Tape It Up**: Have an important recipe you can't lose? Print or write it out and tape it inside a cabinet.
5. **Don't Go-Go Gadget**: Fancy kitchen gadgets can be a waste of time and money. Invest in a set of good knives, skillets and spatulas and you've got a good start. Quality is most important.
6. **First Aid Alert**: Keep a first aid kit in the kitchen pantry. When you have a minor emergency like a cut or burn, you'll appreciate the convenience and close proximity.
7. **Goofy Goggles**: Keep a pair of swim or safety goggles in the kitchen drawer. Wear them when cutting onions to avoid tears.
8. **Chopstick Cleaners**: Save the chopsticks from Chinese takeout. Use them after cooking to scrape hard-to-reach spills from stove and countertop edges without scratching.
9. **Gross But Grate**: If you want a handy, finger-protecting grater, purchase a heel callus and bunion remover with a receptacle to hold scrapings. Ginger, citrus zest, and chocolate can be easily grated and held in the receptacle. Label FOR KITCHEN USE ONLY.
10. **Know Your Knives**: Knives have specific uses. In general, knives with serrated edges cut soft foods with hard crusts. Knives with straight blades are used for cutting and slicing meats and veggies.

11. **The Sharper The Better**: When purchasing kitchen knives, choose the sharpest. It's actually safer and quicker to cut using very sharp knives.

12. **Not Just For Eggs**: Use an egg slicer to slice other tender foods, such as mushrooms, avocados, and kiwis.

13. **Best Burner**: Make sure to choose the best burner for the pan size and meal you are cooking. Your food will cook more efficiently and you'll save energy too.

14. **Pan Particulars**: When cooking large meats in the oven, be careful to choose a sturdy pan with handles. A flimsy pan may mean a meal on the floor rather than on the dinner table.

15. **Cast Iron Seasoning**: To season a cast iron pan, first wash it with hot, soapy water. Scrub using a stiff brush, rinse and dry completely. With a folded paper towel, put a light, even coating of oil around the inside and outside of the pan. Heat the pan on the top oven rack at 350 degrees F for an hour. Allow it to cool inside the oven. Place aluminum foil on the bottom rack for oily drips.

16. **Clean Can Openers**: Can opener blades can get dirty and harbor germs. Scrub blades often using an old toothbrush.

17. **Under Pressure**: For best nutrient retention, the best cooking method is pressure cooking (about 90% of them). Boiling retains the fewest nutrients (about 40%).

18. **Hold The Water**: Pressure cookers need very little water. About one cup of water or liquid should be enough, but check your recipe or manual to be certain.

19. **Nice & Warm**: Want warm plates for a dinner party? Sprinkle with just a little water and place them in the microwave for about 30 seconds. They'll come out slightly warm for serving.

20. **Safer Mixing**: Place a damp, folded kitchen towel under the mixing bowl. This will reduce sliding and improve safety and efficiency.

21. **Clean Grater**: To clean your grater easily, rub a small amount of cooking oil on it before use. Cheeses and other sticky ingredients will wash right off.

Vegan Eating

1. **Plant Power**: Vegan eating can be quite healthy when using nutritious beans, peas, lentils, nuts, and seeds to substitute for meat protein.
2. **Lick The Bowl**: Another good reason to eat vegan is that when you make vegan cookies, you can safely eat the egg-free dough!

Vegetables

1. **Sumptuous Skins**: Vegetables and fruits have the most nutrients and fiber in the skin. So instead of peeling, eat the skins when possible.
2. **Double Dicing**: When a recipe calls for a small portion of onions or peppers, dice a whole one. Store the unneeded portion in a zipper plastic bag in the refrigerator or freezer for future recipes.
3. **Root Veggies**: Cook root veggies like potatoes and carrots with the lid on for a quicker meal.
4. **No More Tears**: Reduce the tears from cutting onions. Place onions in the freezer for 5 minutes before cutting.
5. **Great Greens**: Cut fresh green beans quickly and easily by grasping a bunch in your hand and lining up the ends in your palm. Lay them on a cutting board and cut the knobby ends off. Turn them around and do the same with the other ends.
6. **It's In The Bag**: Create a "scrap" bag in the freezer. Toss in leftover pieces of freshly cut veggies to use later for soups and stir-frying.
7. **Perfect Peas**: Frozen peas don't need to be cooked, only thawed. They can be used at the last minute for salads by thawing in a colander under cool running water.
8. **Hold The Seeds**: Need to seed a cucumber quickly and easily? Cut it lengthwise and run a spoon down the center to scrape out the seeds.
9. **Catching Critters**: When washing fresh garden vegetables, soak them briefly in slightly salty water. Insects dislike the salt and will come out to be washed away.
10. **Longer-Lasting Greens**: For longer-lasting lettuce and celery, remove from plastic bags. Storing them in paper bags makes them last longer.

11. **Core The Lettuce**: Hit the core end of lettuce forcefully on the kitchen counter. The core will loosen and can be pulled out without cutting.
12. **Soften Slow**: When your recipe calls for softening your onions, don't rush the process. Softening onions takes longer than you might think. To do it properly, expect to spend about 20-30 minutes on this step alone.
13. **Fresh Or Dried**: When using fresh herbs, remember that 1 tablespoon of fresh herbs equals 1 teaspoon of dried herbs.
14. **Fresh Onions**: When using green onions, save the white ends to grow fresh. Submerge the ends in a glass of fresh water, place in the sun, and let nature do its job.

Web-Based Cooking Help

1. **Cyber-Cooking**: Try to have a tablet or laptop and Wi-Fi available in the kitchen area. Recipes and cooking tips are a mouse click away!

2. **Creative Comments**: For online recipes, read comments provided by others who have tried the same recipe. Learn from cooks who have already prepared the recipe - they often have improvements!

3. **Smartphone Apps**: Look into smartphone cooking apps. Apps are available to keep up with menu planning, recipes, healthy choices, grocery lists, and more.

More Cooking Tips and Tricks!

1. **Clogged Drains**: To clear clogged drains naturally, combine 1 cup each of baking soda and salt, then slowly pour down the drain. Let it sit for 5 minutes then pour in a pan or teakettle of boiling water. Repeat as needed.
2. **Quick Recipe Book Holder**: Need your hands free for cooking? Use the clip from a pants hanger to keep the pages open.
3. **Perfect Rice**: If you want perfect rice that's not sticky, use lemon juice. Just 2 tablespoons added to the water will keep the grains from sticking together.
4. **Quick Ice Packs**: Need an easy, no-mess ice pack for your child's lunch? Soak a new kitchen sponge in water, place in zipper plastic bag and freeze.
5. **Expanding Ice**: Be careful when freezing foods with high water contents such as soft cheeses, food emulsions, and eggs in the shell. Freezing will change the textures of high-moisture foods; eggshells will crack.
6. **Texture Tip**: Try to add texture to soft foods for contrast. Mashed potatoes? Add some crunchy bacon bits. Creamy guacamole? Top it with lightly salted pumpkin or sunflower seeds.
7. **Pumpkin Scooping**: For quicker and easier seeding of pumpkins and squash, use an ice cream scoop.
8. **Jar Power**: To open a tightly sealed jar lid, place a rubber band around the lid. Wrap with a cloth and turn.
9. **Floss To Cut**: If you need to cut softer foods, a knife can be too damaging. Use unscented/unflavored dental floss to cut soft cheeses and cakes.
10. **Breadcrumbs In A Snap**: Freeze stale bread to grind in a food processor later. It's a quick and easy way to make breadcrumbs when needed.

11. **Clean While You Cook**: Cleaning up as you cook keeps you organized and with ample space.
12. **Ample Storage**: Cooking in bulk is a great way to plan for future meals. However, make sure you have plenty of containers and storage space in the freezer before beginning.
13. **Cool It Down**: Don't place hot food directly in the freezer. Allow it to cool down in the refrigerator first. Placing hot items in the freezer can raise the temperature too much and partially thaw frozen items.
14. **Get Trashy**: When cooking, keep a plastic grocery bag hanging on the outside cabinet door handle. It's a handy way to throw things away quickly without having to open and close the door often.
15. **Soapy Sink**: To encourage quick cleanups as you go, keep your sink filled with hot, soapy water while cooking. You'll be more likely to wash, rinse, and put away quickly.
16. **Animal Instincts**: Trust your senses when cooking. If something doesn't smell right to you, it's probably spoiled.
17. **Read Recipes**: When trying a new recipe, always read it completely first. Avoid the frustration of starting to cook and realizing you are missing an ingredient or utensil!
18. **Guessing Temp & Time**: If you're unsure of how long to cook something, cooking it at lower heat for a longer time is best. You're less likely to burn your meal.
19. **Prep Ahead**: When cooking a big meal, do as much as you can ahead of time. Cutting vegetables, making stock, and measuring spices can all be done ahead.
20. **Cool Cream**: To whip cream faster and more efficiently, chill the cream, the bowl and the beaters first.
21. **Cinnamon Surprise:** Surprise your guests with an added flavor in your whipped cream. Add a dash each of cinnamon and nutmeg to whipped cream as it's being prepared.

22. **Fake Funnel**: When you need a funnel but don't have one handy, roll up a paper plate. Or snip off a corner of a mailing envelope and use the cone shape as a funnel.
23. **Perfect Liquids**: When measuring liquids, always measure on a flat, stable surface. Trying to measure while holding the cup may lead to inaccurate measurements.

Want More?

For more great tips and other books, visit
TopBooksToday.com

Printed in Great Britain
by Amazon

34697479R00047